WEAVES OF TIME

WEAVES OF TIME

Pages from a Poetic Diary

Sangeeta Gupta

PARTRIDGE
A Penguin Company

ISBN: Softcover   978-1-4828-1033-2
            Ebook   978-1-4828-1034-9

Partridge books may be ordered through booksellers or by contacting:

Partridge India
Penguin Books India Pvt.Ltd
11, Community Centre, Panchsheel Park, New Delhi 110017
India
www.partridgepublishing.com
Phone: 000.800.10062.62

DEDICATION

For Tanmaya & Deepali,
two grounded in truth.

CONTENTS

FOREWORD

In this volume of poems, subtitled—pages from a poetic diary—we have, often enough at any rate, a fresh re-enactment of a hoary cultures, one key preoccupation, namely, the search for the self, and that whether in its micro or macro dimensions. The diurnal world is not ignored in the body of the poems, but this more modest aspect of a multifaceted reality is never observed from on high, with a cold eye, but with due affection. On the other hand it is the poet's own first personal singular voice that is treated almost with a clinical detachment. Here the speaking voice makes of itself an object, but one that still needs to be raised to the level of a true, self-scrutinizing subject, freed of its infirmities, its grosser attributes. For only by doing so may a mortal draw a millimeter closer to whatever is termed as divinity. Divinity is instinct in all creatures, but its true emergence from the midst of the Kurukshetra of workaday life can only happen after untold inner dialogues, of self with soul. Both these last two words are tryingly vague, but any who tend the acres of their inner landscape, free it of its weeds; they thus know that the soul comes about only by their incessant labor, that of a life-long conversation between the I and the me, between I and the thou, and that it is only so that consciousness gives birth to conscience. It is in some such way that the human creature rises a few cubits.

In sum, it is to all such life action, emotion and vision that the poet fastidiously works to gives form. The strategies or the choices that she employs in her quintessential lines are not mere rhetoric, they convince us that for her the making of verse is not an end in itself, but that it is as well a means of remaking of our being. This especial stance is of value in our value bereft times. The poet, sufficiently aware of our present shortfalls, takes us on a meaningful journey via her diary. Health of spirit is the main goal to which her finger unerringly points out.

KESHAV MALIK
Poet & Art Critic

I

With you Time
dramatizes into diamonds
into pearly moments.

Nay, I do not 'spend time',
with you, I weave it
into a poem, a painting.

II

Time?—time
Is an abstract notion
you can almost do
what you like with it

you can even recreate it
so flexible it

you can make time timeless—
waste it too—
it changes with your each mood

it can be sad,
be cheerful
not it your master
it is your obedient slave, you can
tame it.

a powerful tool—
to you given as gift,
to be used as you wish.

you it is, who it perceives
you who decide its fate.

you who,
it has got to serve.

III

In this post-noon solitude
a playful sun
kisses your eyes
but softly so
and then instead
of weaving dreams
you weave silence

The inner fire is ready
as though to explode
like a playful butterfly

The rebel is reborn
as if looking for a new horizon
to grow in—for
an awareness near total,
for not else
but reconnect
to re-bond
to be sheerly,

so you are
alive each moment
alive here and now
and for as long
as ever is.

IV

Love is so abstract
it is of no guaranteed definition

Each one defines it differently

You can feel
its there somewhere
between earth and space
may be all over

words fail

it can be understood
only in the completest of silence
indeed it is hid in the innermost core
of an elusive existence

Touch core
and it you will know.

V

In this
sunkissed afternoon
I realize
you are often
in my thoughts

the warmth of the
soft velvet sun
also has
the warmth
of your deep recall

VI

evening—
filled with your laughter—
suddenly makes me realize
I am alive, that I am talking to myself
that life itself is
the key poem.

VII

In an utter silence
I hear you
hear the unsaid
hear that
which never touched
your lips
I hear feelings
which are hidden
secreted with utmost care
in the in-most
bole of your being

the pure, the raw truth
is not spoilt,
nor expressed
in words
which have lost
their meanings
in this, so utter a silence
sans communication, sans connection

yet see
how still I hear you
understand you completely.

VIII

It is now I can grasp
the silence—
appreciate
the steep beauty,
the bliss of what is not

The sound and fury inside
vanishing
and the void is replate
with the gong of silence

each moment of this same supreme quiet
making you grounded
in the here and now—
of no sound
only song.

IX

As artist
I wish to paint nought else
but pin-drop silence

wish to weave
the texture of that special sound
that is unheard

wish to share with you
this, an element out of ear-shot,
on the blank of a canvas

silence
so abstract

well, you may feel it
but not define it
for words just cannot express
what is rare

strange
that one can sense,
it, that is simply unsaid.

X

When is silence, when speechlessness
a poem's kin?

I know it in my bones
its really the roll back
of the tide of times
we spent together,
times that seemed timeless
those so secretly stored
in the invisible most pore
of ones being

the joy of knowing without being told—
bliss of understanding,
the satisfaction
of being understood without strain
minus speech
and once more one is aware,
of a Presence
during when the molten silver of silence
flows like a poem,
like a flowing pen.

XI

A glorious day
slowly crosses
the river of a misty evening
only to dissolve
in a mysterious night
and I go through it
all the way

may be, as part of it—
but at the same time
only a witness to it—
of the magical happening

In deep silence
I talk to me
Who am I?
The real I?
one who, of it is part
or perchance
simply one witnessing
that same *it?*

and in my heart of hearts
I answer
may it be I just know
I am both

A universe that exists in me
and I
in that very universe.

XII

Adam,
an evolved being, dove-tailed into a whole,
by nature stands alone
on the crossroads
to create life afresh
the life of his choice,
as a being, not just thing.

Though it's always easy,
secure and comforting
to follow the proven path
still one is also given the choice
to carve only an own path
to walk on and on
on an uncertain, unknown terrain

to explore in the freedom,
the invention of an own destiny,
to avail the opportunity
of a vertical take off

to transform the mundane
heat and fret
into blazing night light.

XIII

The Creator
Of creators
has gifted humankind
the choice
of hewing his own life

so go ahead
create a day by far beautiful,
indeed so
each moment of your life,
to enjoy this lucky freedom of choice.

make own path
alone walk
that One
always holds
your solitary hand
nay is always
part of your beating heart

so creative be
it makes the maker
proud of thee.

XIV

a lazy
unstructured Sunday:
the luxury of
going for a walk.

The humming bees of silence,
the enjoying of my all alone time

the dew on wet grass
looks happy
perhaps being sunkissed
on this, the wintery morning.

Sun making every shivering being
live after the cold, dark,
impersonal night.

XV

Time disappears
come the hour
of tight-lipped silence,
then when no sound is
only stillness

no noise even of any thought,
absolute bliss it is
for once you are not amiss,
but centered in your
crucial life-cell
and as to realize
you are
complete by yourself

by yourself—you?
yes you a whole Universe.

XVI

Only in an unfractured silence
can one thrive
there then is no wandering mind,
no sound, no noise,
no thought
no past,
no future nor

Time only in the moment is.
So aware be
of each passing moment
time, time only in the present is—
no not
in no past, no future.

in that moment alone joy,
alive like the crazy
honey-drunk bee

XVII

I, on a journey
so inward
so intimate,
so personal am

so all by my singular self
in sea-deep silence,
that it helps
materialize me—
to actualize
my utmost possibility.

Now am I aware
Me, myself, I can transform
can redirect the flow of a life-line—mine,
and that the
gift of choice is
given each one
to become aware

Life, that one gift
of the choice to be,
of creativity.
Miracle
without a parallel.

XVIII

Have thee realized!
are thee aware!
that even as we meet
there is, of energies
a concordance,
an inter-play
of minds, in the air; in bubbling chemistry

a rhythm, a solace, and a peace,
yea, the very celebration of cosmos

Ah me, for me
these meetings are tidings
worth waiting for,
and for much more?

XIX

When the like minded meet
a miracle shall happen:
the you and the I
be hugely recharged, be revived, rejuvenated,

each time
we are gathered together
I instantly sense
an intense energy field
tightly encompassing us.

there is, then, as though magic in the air
laughter in hearts
music in our mutual souls
life feels, life reels

oh, my own twin.

XX

I was musing
will our evenings be yet
as magical as when
we were close together

Well,
I can almost read my poems
when I look into your eyes

I hear music in the air
when you are around
then is there laughter
there then joy
there timelessness abounding
in the bonding.

XXI

wish I could carve you
on the palm
of my hand,
carve you
as my one and only destiny!

wishes are,
alas, nought
but wistful thinkings.

Inspite of this being so
how I wish to carve
a destiny.

Am told, that,
I perforce am given this choice

Oh, pray why?
For am I not destiny's own child
and you
that very destiny are.

XXII

You
my reincarnation seem,
seem my mirror image
and that even
while I am
not yet gone.

I wonder, though,
how such things transpire!
I speak to self, say
that once in a while
magic will come about,
though not known how

Remember,
there is a gap of decades
between our two births
on this top-like whirling planet
and still I am dogged,
namely that you are none other
than my twin
I over and over speak to self, tell:
that at all times, miracles and magics
will happen.

XXIII

My hip hip hurray baby has grown
to be a man
and so now not to be cuddled
nor, no more for it the lullaby
to make him sleep deep

But then he still is
the greatest of God gift to me—
a best friend—
my best, the most creative craft
masterpiece
lifeline
as serves
my biggest source of strength
true inspiration
my reason to be.

Some things in life—
do what you like—
just do not change
even with the passage of time,
that headlong running thief.

XXIV

For a change,
this evening, I don't have
a "to do list" tagged to it

so, unplanned, un-structured
I decide to scan
newspaper
listen to music
perhaps to do nothing
but only to realize to my utter surprise
that a kind of sadness
has crept up inside me,
and that as well a sense
of sea-deep emptiness.
I search unknowingly
and suddenly stop
and of self ask
is doing something
or the other
all time—
seemingly mindful
still mindless?
is it to drop dead,
hit bed post in deep slumber

the purpose of living?—
The question lingers long in my hurrying heart

is this then the goal and purpose
of life!— any life?

XXV

Life kept searching—
a whole night—for me

it kept searching my dreams
asked about my whereabouts

Life even inquired from
the dark night,
but none could help.

Life kept on the look out for me
night after night quite desperate
only to realise
that I was lost
entangled in
the sun-struck rays
of an arising dawn.

XXVI

The mounting morning mist
surely is the manifestation
of Nature's very own
non-stop symphony

the soft music
of the breeze reaches me
and after a meeting with you
we both—
born after a divide of decades—
are still twins
of that one timeless
moment
where souls lock
beyond body and belief.

Love has its own dialect
not expressed except in fine feelings

words spoil
loves purity
without fail

hear, silence alone
manifests love
better than the lines
of all my poems.

XXVII

Eating samosa?-
Oh that, of taste-buds,
no mere indulgence;
a ritual, rather,
of rememberances
of memories
as fresh as
morning dew.

My evenings were once filled
with the steaming samosas
you brought
and I, always,
could see a samosa
transform from inane
to metaphysical—
abstract, and so ephemeral
as love.

You are not here more
so now I buy that one
once in a while
eat it, with a smile
as ritual
in the elation of what was.

XXVIII

Sitting in my dingy studio—
listening to
the song of songs—
of silence—
the trees outside window
dancing
with the breeze
as if they all had a bath
in the rain
last night
while I slept.

In deep slumber
I could not hear
the whispers . . . .
you were unfailingly sending me
in your dreams all through.

Oh but
I prefer to stay away
from all night dreams
for do I not dream throughout
the day!

I? I'm the perpetual
day dreamer.

XXIX

Love is self attrition
it comes with a package—
of hurt and pain

when love does happen
hurt and pain
are not far away.

Fully aware,
one still craves
that one sheer magic,
it that gives each a heady feel

Its fire, as singes
a passion
as destroys completely—
makes of one a poet
of another a painter, or anything you name
thus devastated, and destroyed,
one still Becomes . . . . a being
enriched and entranced.
And this is no paradox.

If you have not yet
suffered love
how could you
have lived?

XXX

I die each day
and yet am reborn again
come day.

All hurts, shames,
all humiliations, all sorrows
die with me come morn.

In my reincarnations
I have a selective, knife-keen memory!

But forget not
I only remember love
and its blessings.

XXXI

I loose sense come night
though only to wake up every sun-break
with a fresh discovery: Me.

It is the day's challenge
to know this one
and I'm dying to explore
an ever strange new me, day after day

This alone is for me life—
this journey
is for me to meet me
but only to loose that one;
to meet it once again
and so it goes on and on, and on.

XXXII

Life's biggest hurdle?
to understand and comprehend
your own tiny dot called self

Yet I do not expect to be understood,
that is,
since I have not even
understood my own allotted life-cell.

XXXIII

You always beautiful were,
spring doing wonders
to your secret beauty
you ever sit in the lap of history—
proud yet elegant
you give the gift
of immense possibilities,
infinite opportunities
to each and all
who seek,

so to me you gave
roots to grow and to bloom in,
wings to fly,
you made me feel
that I was deserving of your hospitality

I was welcomed here
and you sustained me
for long years of a ceaseless wrestle

I survive
all because you were there by my side
you it was who gave me cognition, as recognition
made me what I presently am
to you I belong
Oh! City by the yamuna banks
how can I,
you, not adore!

XXXIV

Love is a prolonged growth
the more it grows,
the deeper it

Butterfly kinds
never experience love.
Before love grows its roots even
away they fly.

Butterfly kinds suffers perpetually—
neither to love
nor to be loved

Butterfly kinds
lay love waste.

XXXV

Love is to be accepted
with utmost grace

Most are
so afraid, insecure so
love they escape.
Too powerless to love,
of being loved incapable.

If escape is a state of mind—
that is, when you shun suffering—
you as well escape love, escape life

Own love, accept life
every moment nothing less,
and then
alive, alive, alive
is all there is

XXXVI

One can never pray—
oh no,
for that is not an act,
but a ritual
to be performed
in silence absolute

no noise,
monologue none
a second when your pit-patting heart
becomes a gesture, a prayer—
the prayer of true care

XXXVII

Constant the conversation
through the flux of text messages
and you are no more there,
nor do I exist
in your eye-view

oh even though being right there
besides you.

I was then with a self —mine own—
and enjoyed what was mine.

For this I didn't need you at all
the said meeting, hence, was futile,
heavy on time's heart.

Oh! the waste of moments—
those the mortal's precious pearls.

XXXVIII

You may stay
away from me—
choice all yours.

Though,
I keep you safe
in my thoughts,
in my infectious laughter
as in my poems
and in my paintings,
in prayers

you are part and parcel,
an inseparable,
of my being and becoming.

XXXIX

Toasted your tall triumphs
with my one and only friend
who came laughing into my fervent prayers
said
blessed you are,
I come to meet with you
as do all pals.

XXXX

What is learned
through the roll-call of education,
well may have to be unlearned
through meditation.
for not else, not otherwise
can you change a dire fate.

Difficult alright,
yet so
only till you do not decide.

With decision, begins change.
this happens, and the universe helps.
It is possible then to alchemise the crude ore to gold.
Take own responsibility for what or who you are
and change is on the cards.
Well it is your choice,
for have you not a hidden power right within!

Carve then your destiny, I say,
as one does a bread slice.

XXXXI

Death is born
with life, most like a twin.
Like a bamboo-shoot
grows with life it does,
life itself reaches its peak in death.

XXXXII

Say nay to violence
give respect to self
say yea to dignity
say yea to life.

You deserve to live
with self pride.

Mistake not
we all make mistakes
take wrong decisions
once in a while.
Oh, it is all right
to accept failure
in relationships
and to move on
with life.

Never say no to the light of life.
Its this, the chief gift to you,
so use it well.

always
life must be on the go—
be an act of faith.

XXXXIII

Don't punish yourself
for taking a wrong decision.
we all have a right
to make those and then re-learn.

Trusting and loving someone,
who did not deserve our commiseration
is a small mistake,
yourself forgive for it.
Be kind, to self,
we all have to learn
to love ourselves.

Life is to be lived
Moment to moment.
just looking back at the past
is not to respect
the new moment.
which is constantly to be preferred
so we live.

Accept the most high's gift of each split-second
and live it well.
That alone is thanks giving
to the One that really counts.

XXXXIV

poems are candles
which burn
at both ends
so that on certain days
the dark world's dark
is brightened
if just for a second.

If this happens,
even for a wee-flicker, a passing flash
it will make
life and living worth it;

this one heart—mine— is swollen
with some such hope.
So it is I pen,
poems.

XXXXV

Time will
carry away my existence
if though I leave behind
some few poems, some paintings
which may or may not be of interest to anyone

it may be I will be born again
and then what?
I will read those same poems
admire those same paintings.
The idea certainly fascinates me
I will traverse time,
and space, as this birth
and this death
to a stage come back,
come back to these poems and paintings.

They do not belong to me
but I to them.

XXXXVI

In the process of
rediscovering me myself
who did I find?

none but you,
my seeming mirror image

in loving you
is like loving myself.

XXXXVII

When one paints
one penetrates a deep-well—
that of the sub-conscious,

and connects to
one's unconscious,
uncovers one's self,
seeks to know who one is
and in the process
breaks bonds,
liberates one's chained spirit.

Is it not so?
Approach the farthest
and you are connected to the cosmos

you? a nowhere, a nobody!
and yet how still you are, to persist

you belong to the Whole,
that we, the Universe call.

XXXXVIII

Even as one paints,
one as well meditates
transcends, transforms, transmutes

As you create, you die
but then you are reborn,
though you cannot be,
what you were.

You are some other.
Yet folks try to find
the old you, and thus fail.

You are reborn,
with memory none.
You scale time and space.
You are not there, or here,
you die and you are come
beyond time, beyond space.

XXXXIX

Shrouded in darkness,
in silence wrapped,
lying on bed
I, the inner being feel.
And so my heart swells
with a deep sense of gratitude.
to realize that
the creative one
can see what none may,
hear what none will hear.
What more can one want
what more is possible
to be so elate?

In that one still moment
one knows—
Knows that you your energy most conserve
and then to explode it
in your creativity
like a fire-work.

You are still,
very silent.

Like salt
you dissolve,
in your own energy pool
only to be reborn
again and yet again.

XXXXX

We,
dasas of time
are provided with
a cycle of twenty four hours.

Challenge to one's own
is how we create more
of a self, as of passion
from this very daily cycle,
is how we create each moment
of compassion.

Timeless be, I say,
within time.

Fly beyond it,
inscribe your own zone.
break each boundary, liberate,
be a high flying kite.

XXXXXI

Desire is bondage!
So empty be,
be bare space.
Desire, a barrier,
and so even the One
One cannot be desired.

That One will be yours,
will explode,
in infinite energy within you
if only, of desire, you are done.

Let your emptiness
be with the unknown filled,
filled with the mystery,
so sweetness of divinity
enters you.

XXXXXII

The day
you will be
happy with being a self-less self,
that day you will be grounded
in the *here and now*,
and silence sound like a poem.

The season of the present
will thus play the music of spring.

The day you will be content—
your own palms
filled with nothing—
that one day you will smile most lovingly
at your own appearance,

The and only that day you will become
aware of who you are,
and then come
the scented bloom.

XXXXXIII

I existed,
I was there—
there since eternity.
Oblivious of me
I searched for the "I"
all over the seas,
from earth to sky—
I seemed to be part of what Is,
yet did not just
belong there.
I was discovered
but that alone during
my journey deep within.

XXXXXIV

I begged for time
to be with you
but time did not comply

So no more do I,
but carve on my own,
sculpt and paint
and make for you room.

This one time is timeless,
indefinite, surely infinite.
Has scale none, no boundary
no limits, no cycle, zone none
I have crossed endless time
to be nowhere, only with you.

XXXXXV

Creation leaves
no space for tedium
One is surely inventive
but in small change.
One does not seek,
has no goal, no ambition.
One already is
what one wants to be.

Fragrance of deep fulfillment
Lingering all through.

One absorbs the universe
in deep receptivity,
pours
whatever is absorbed
in one's sponge of imagination.

When one surpasses
self, only then
one is closest
the whirling Whole.

Here the poet's first person singular voice is treated almost with clinical detachment. But if it thus makes of itself an object, it is nevertheless raised to the level of a true, self scrutinizing subject, freed of its infirmities, the grosser attributes. Indeed only by doing so may a human draw a millimeter closer to whatever is termed as divinity.

Now 'divinity' is certainly instinct in all creatures, but its true emergence from the midst of the Kurukshetra of workaday life can only happen after untold inner dialogues, of self with soul. These - self and soul - last two words are tryingly vague, but any who tend the acres of their inner landscape, free it of its weeds; they thus know that whatever is termed soul comes about only by incessant labor, that of a life-long conversation between the I and the me, between I and the thou, and that it is only so that an awakened consciousness gives birth to conscience. It is in some such way that the human creature rises a few cubits.

In sum, it is on such life action, emotion and vision that the poet fastidiously works to give form. The strategies or the choices that she employs in her quintessential lines are not mere rhetoric, they convince us that, for her, the making of verse is not an end in itself alone, but that it is as well a means of remaking of our being. This especial stance is of utmost value in our value bereft times. The poet, sufficiently aware of our present shortfalls, takes us on a meaningful journey via her diary. Health of spirit is the main goal to which her writing finger unerringly points out.

Sangeeta Gupta (born Gorakhpur, UP) is a poet, artist and film maker. She has authored a collection of short stories (Nagfani Ke Jungle) and four anthologies of poems (Antas Se, Iss Paar Uss Paar, Samudra Se Lautati Nadi & Pratinaad – translated in English, German, Bangla). Editor of several books and magazines, her paintings are part of the volume 'Visions & Illumination' by Keshav Malik. She represented India in the 9th World Hindi Conference (2012) at Johannesburg.

PARTRIDGE
A Penguin Company

ISBN 978-1-4828-1033-2
90000
9 781482 810332

The Fugitive Sunshine

Selected Poems

SYEDA AFSHANA